Chinese Girls

Hot Sexy Chinese Lingerie Girls Models Pictures

By **PHOTO ART LOVER**

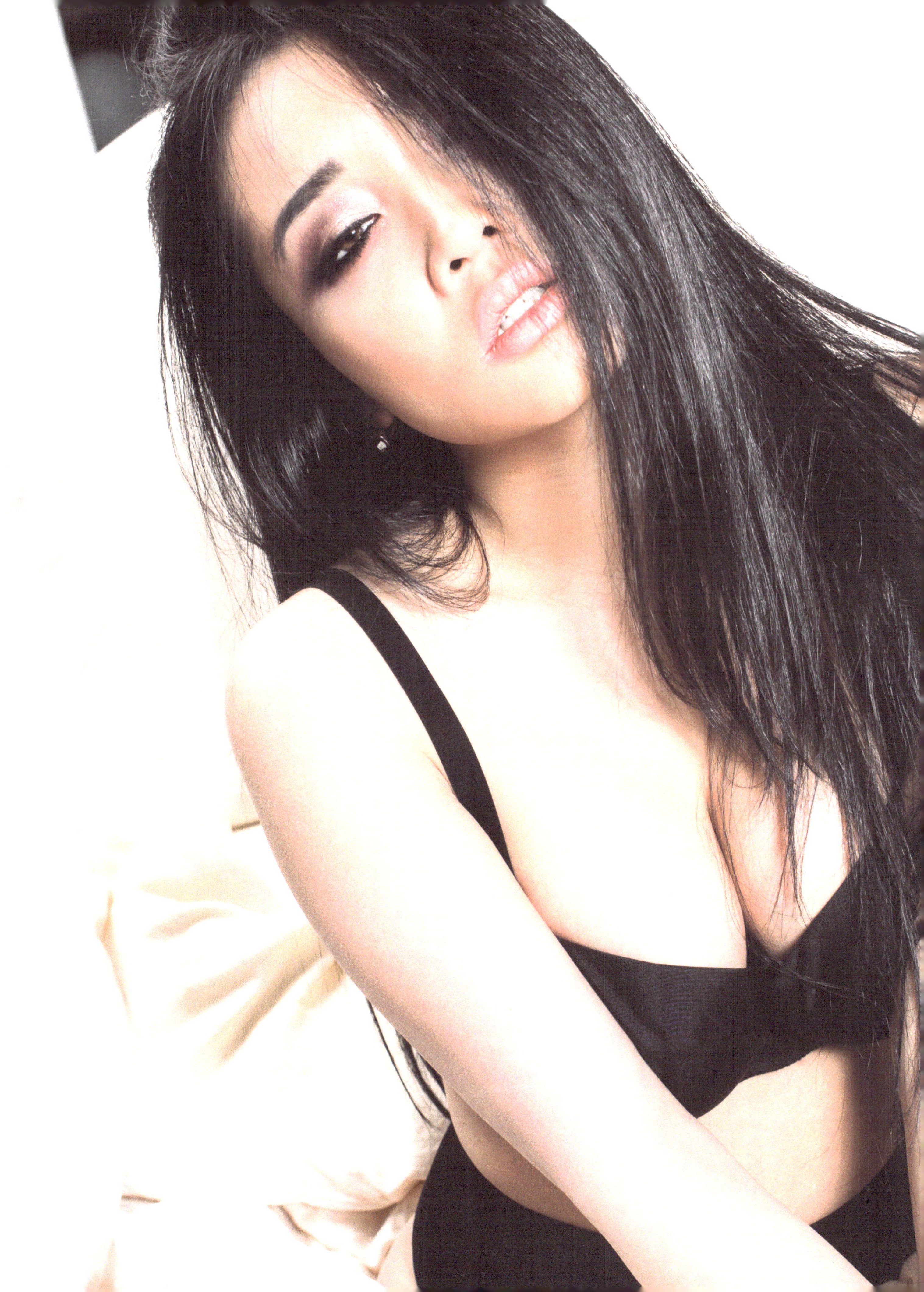

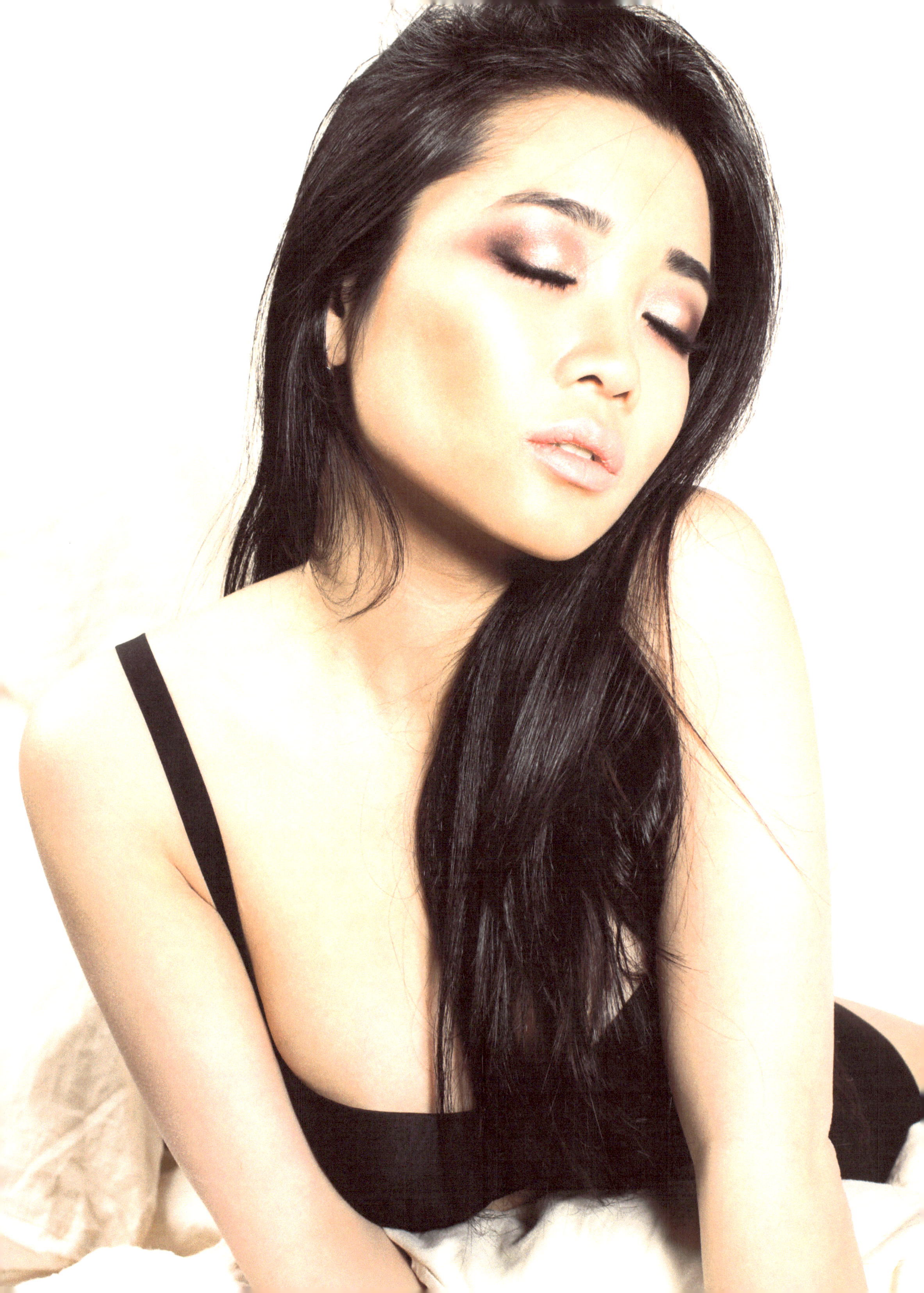

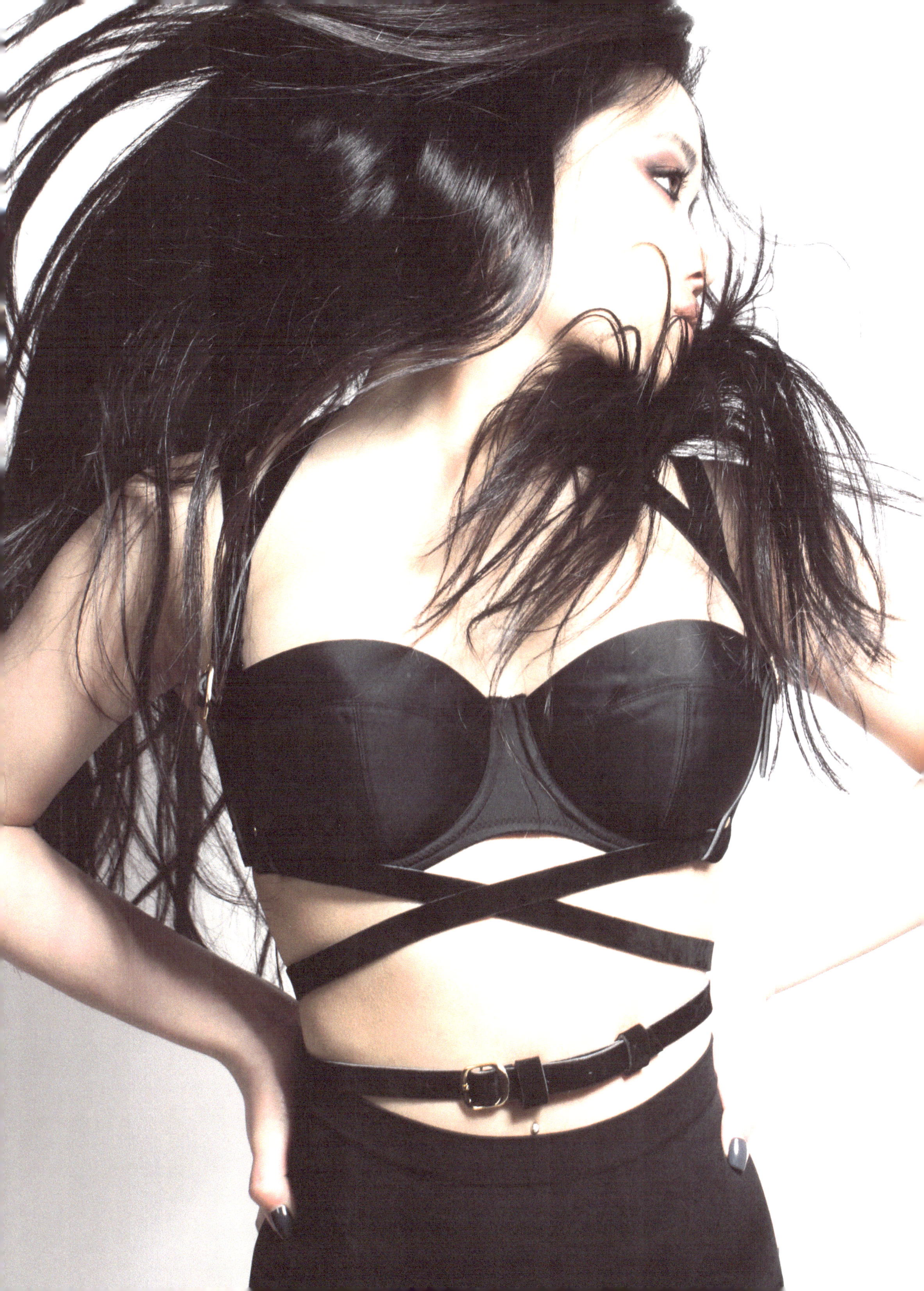

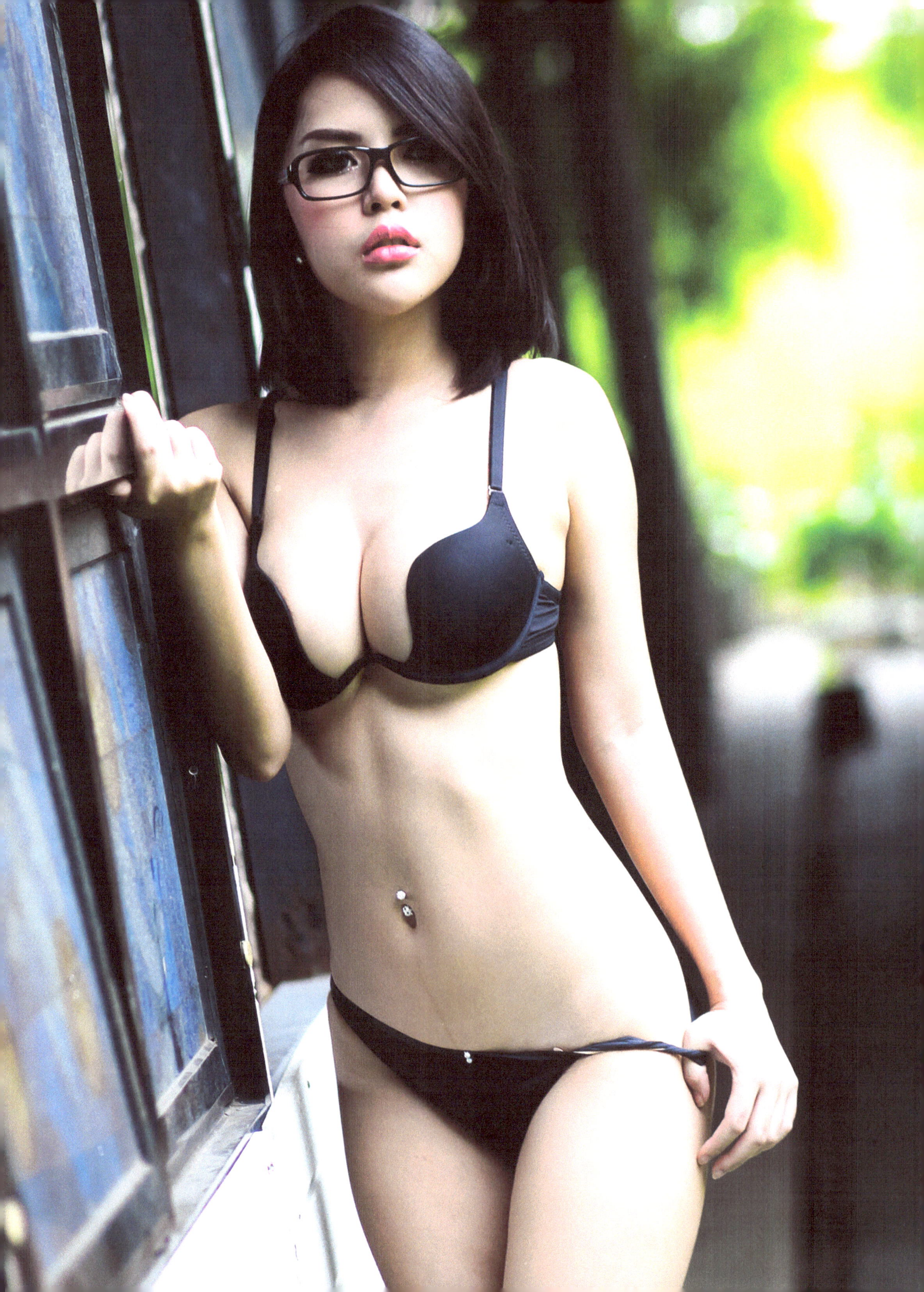

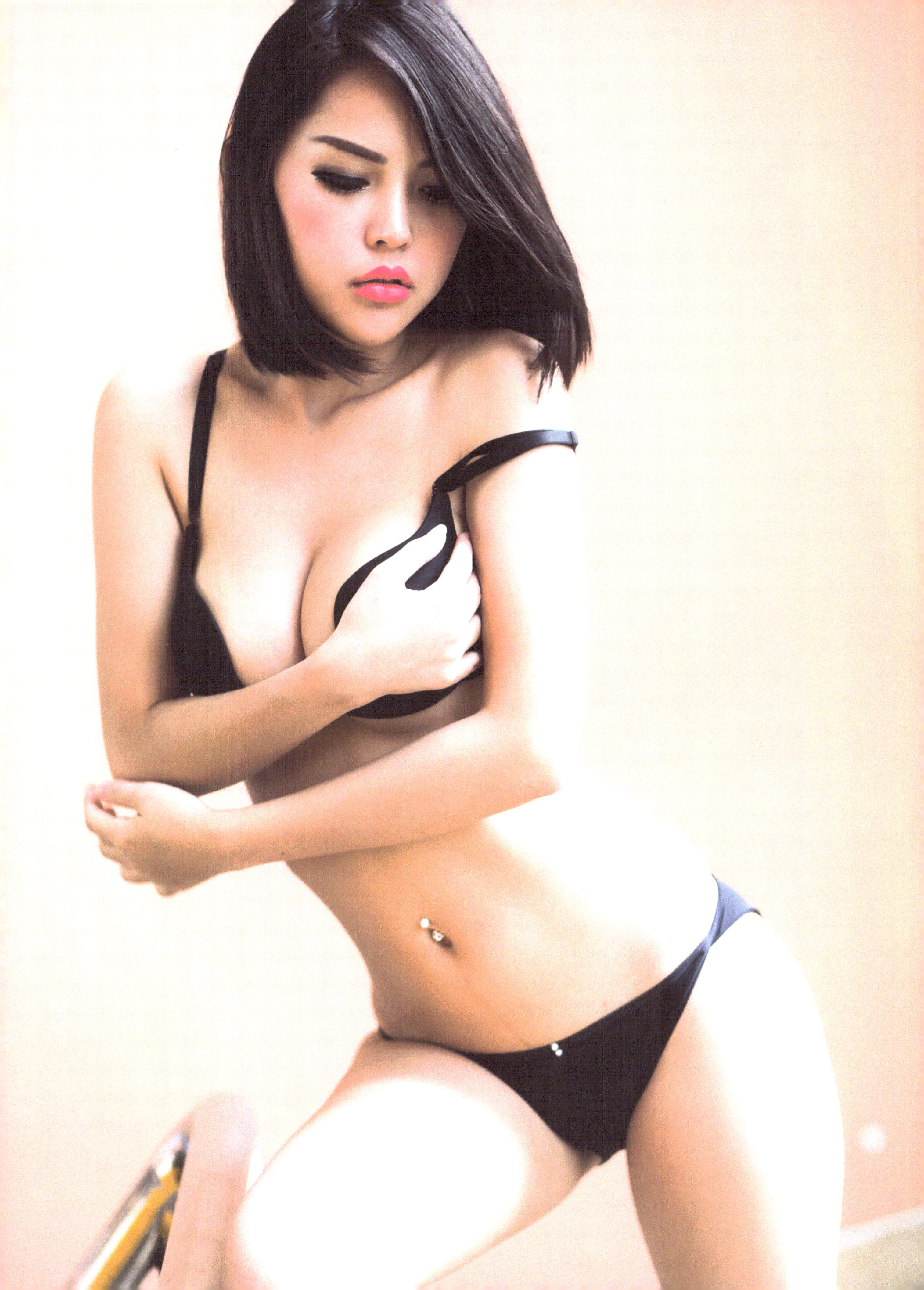

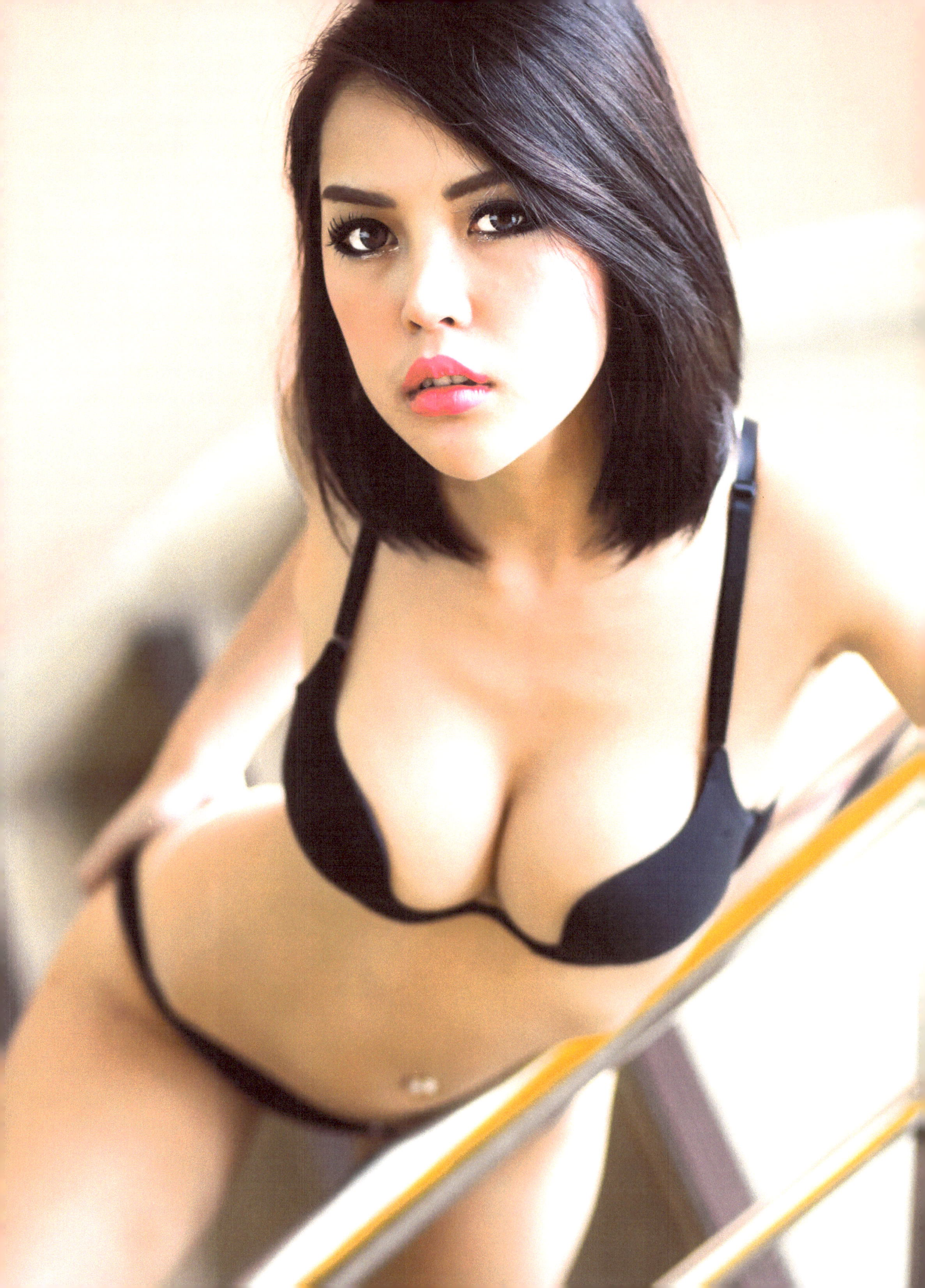

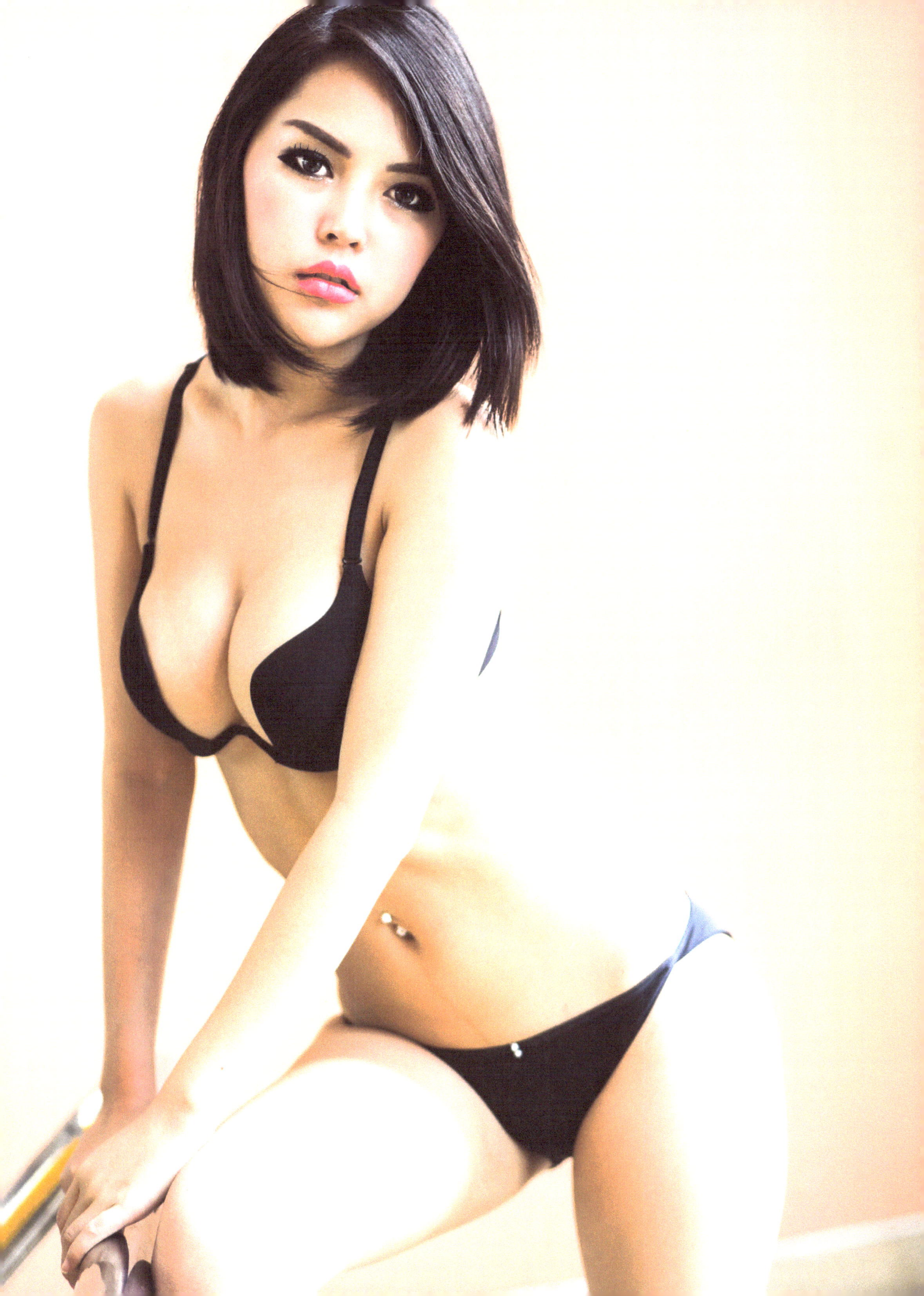

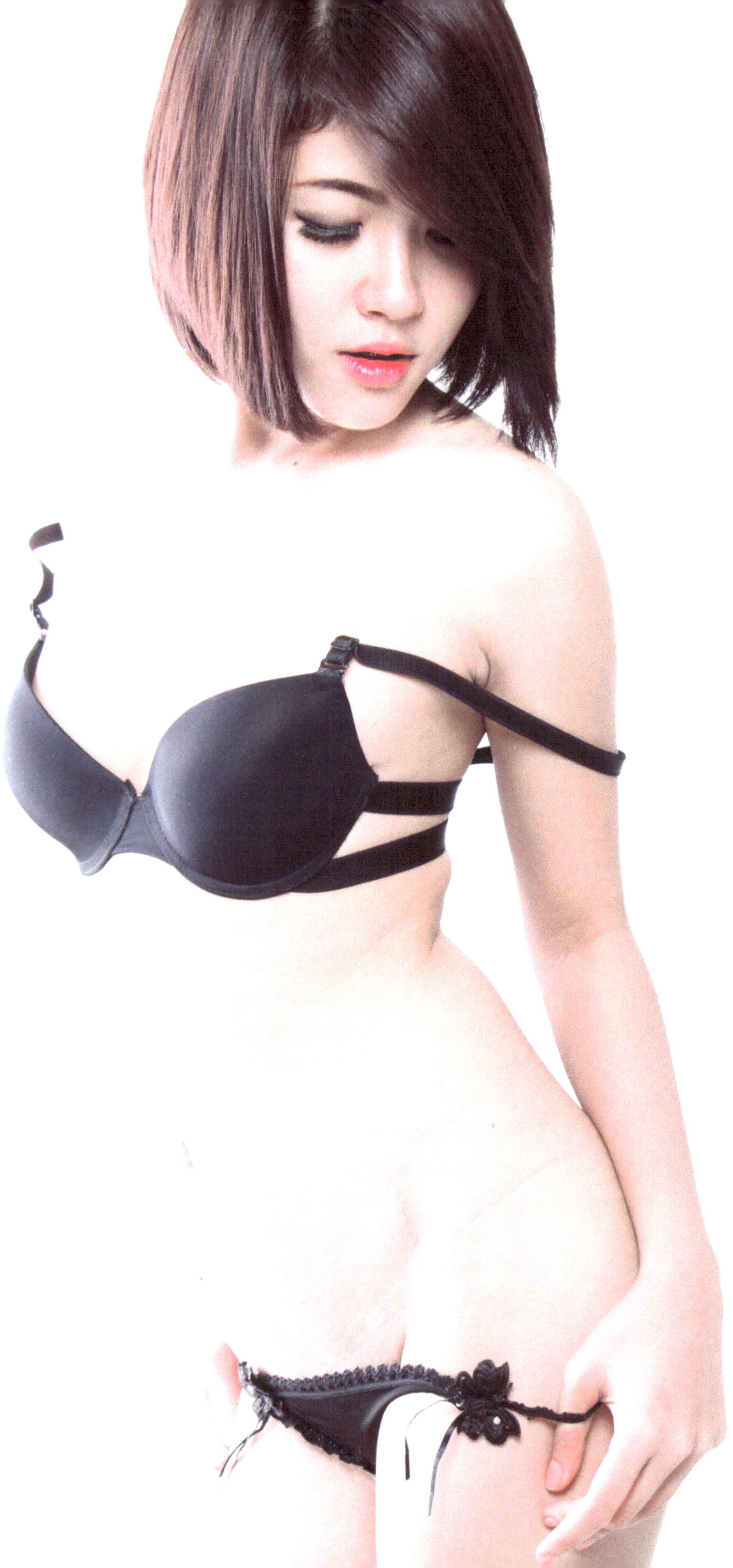

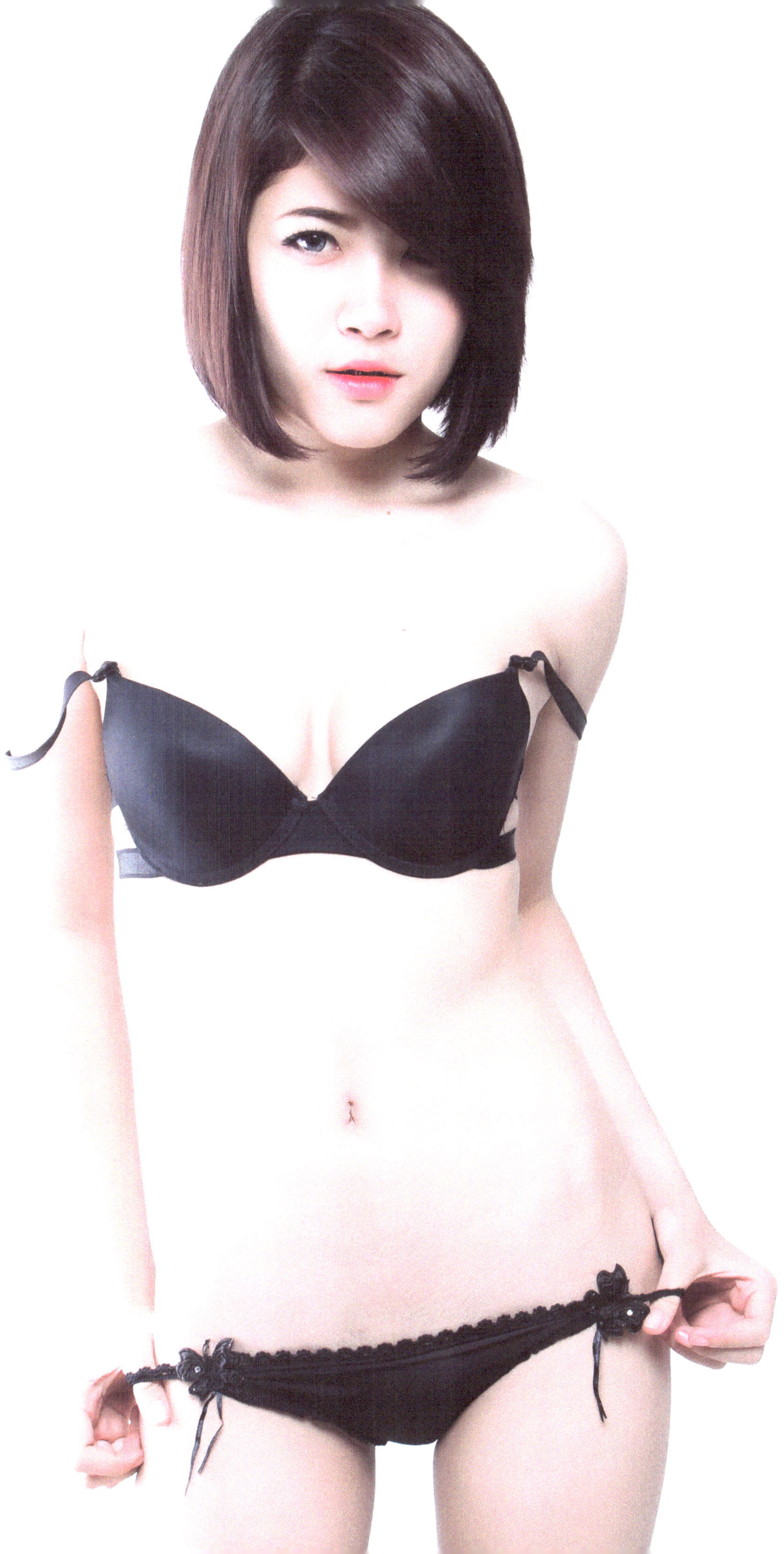

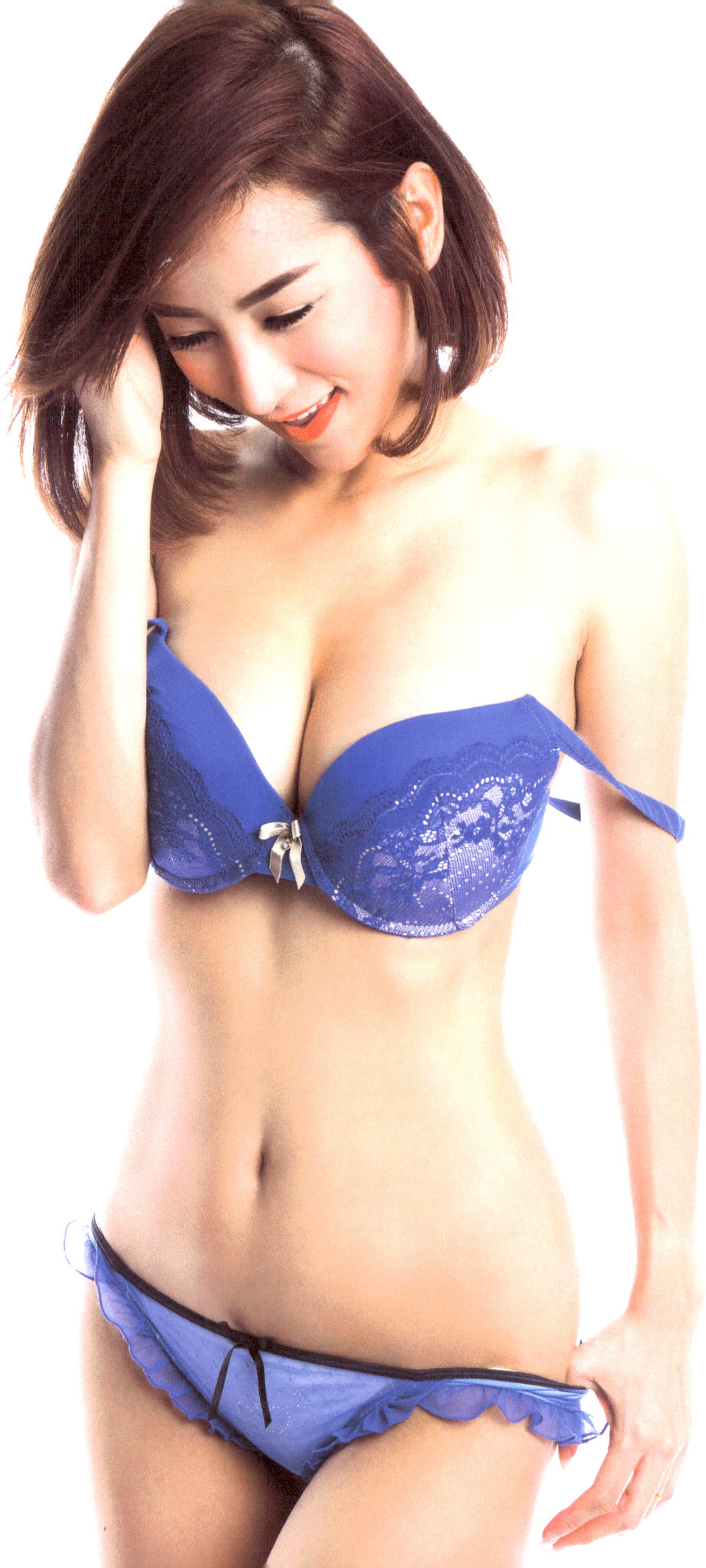

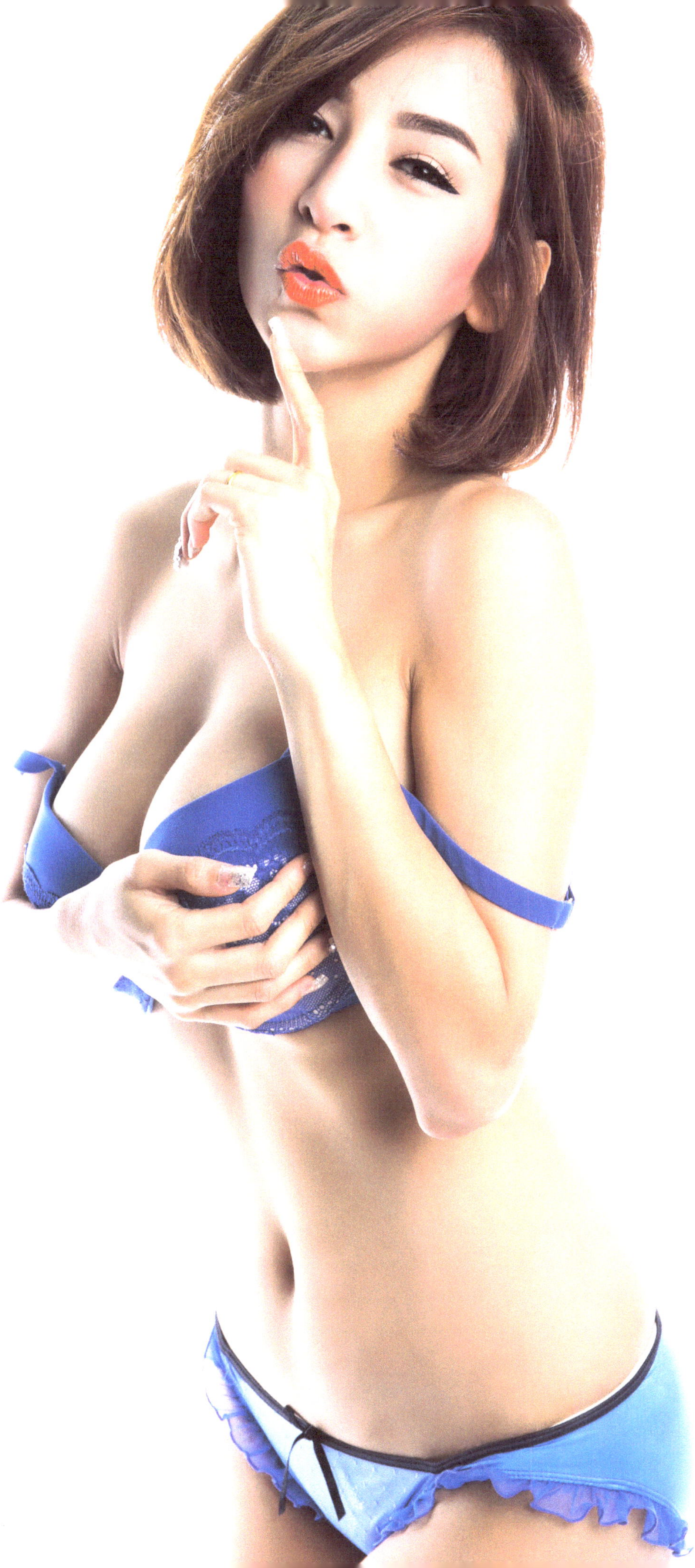

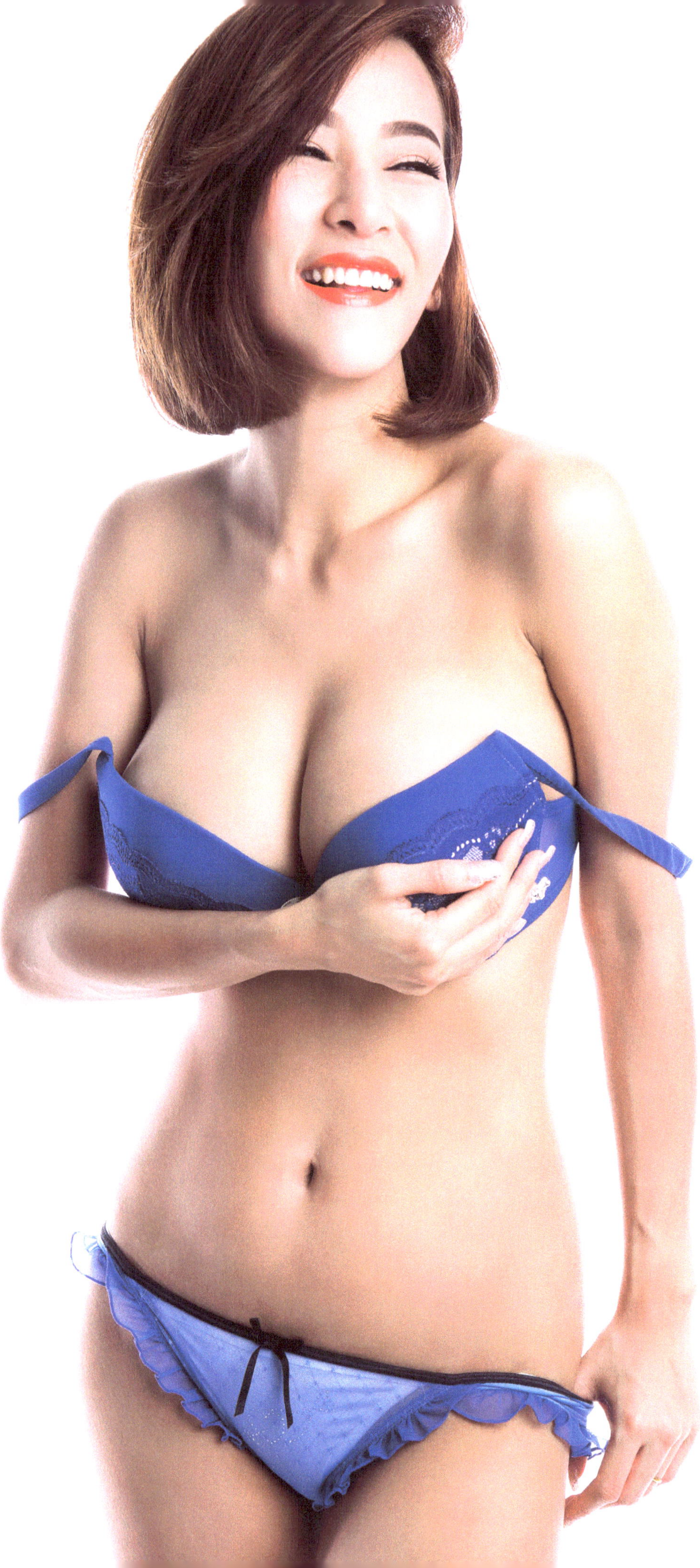

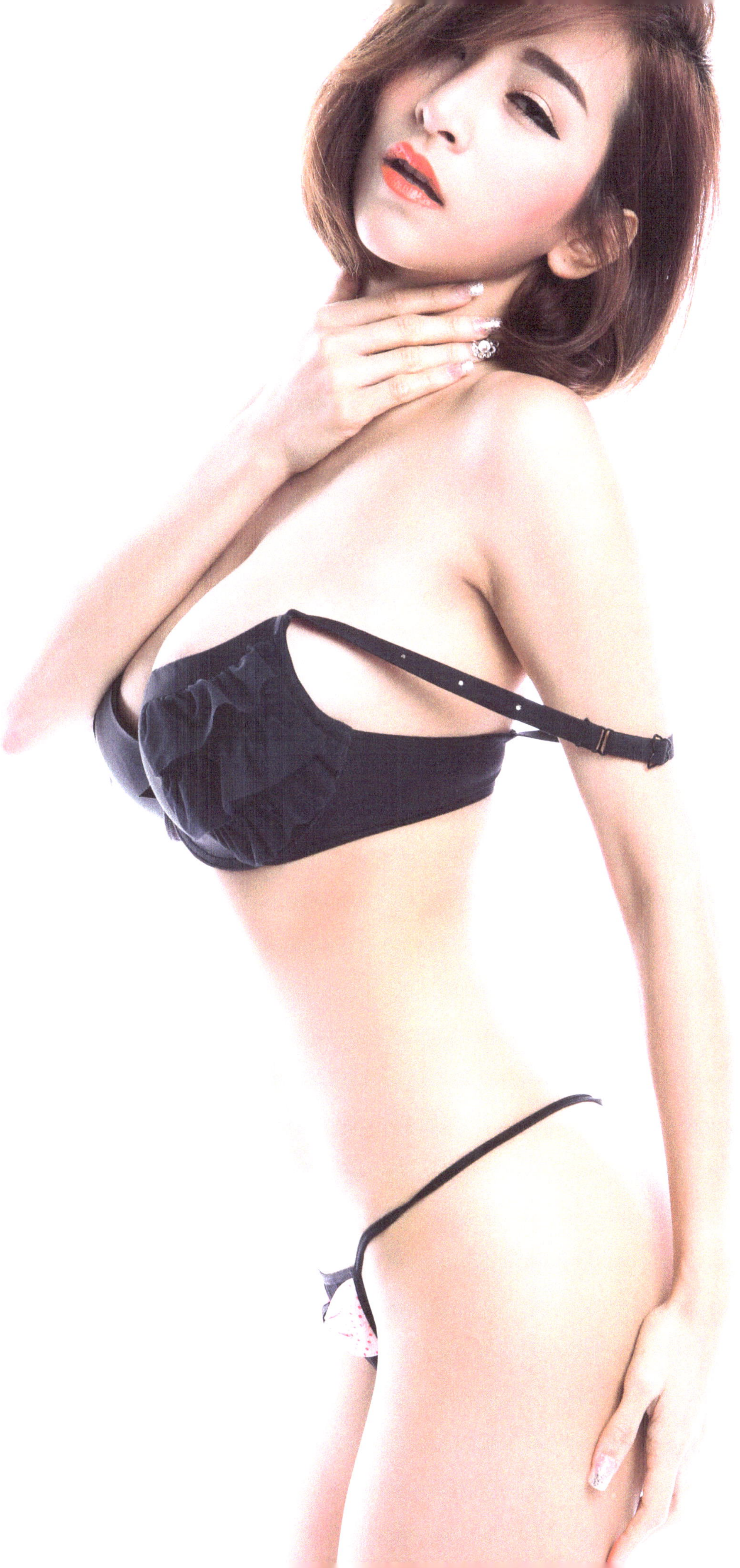

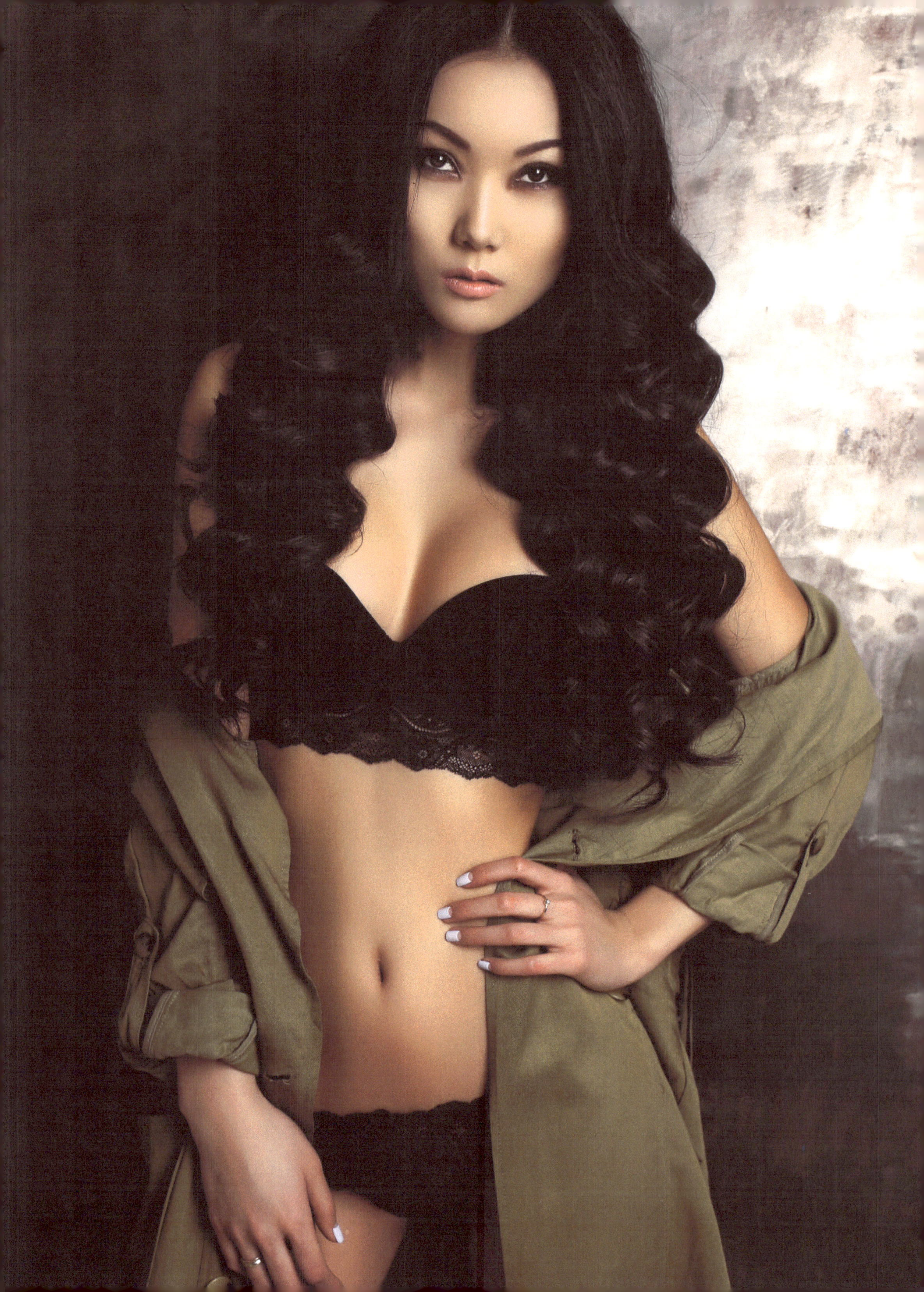

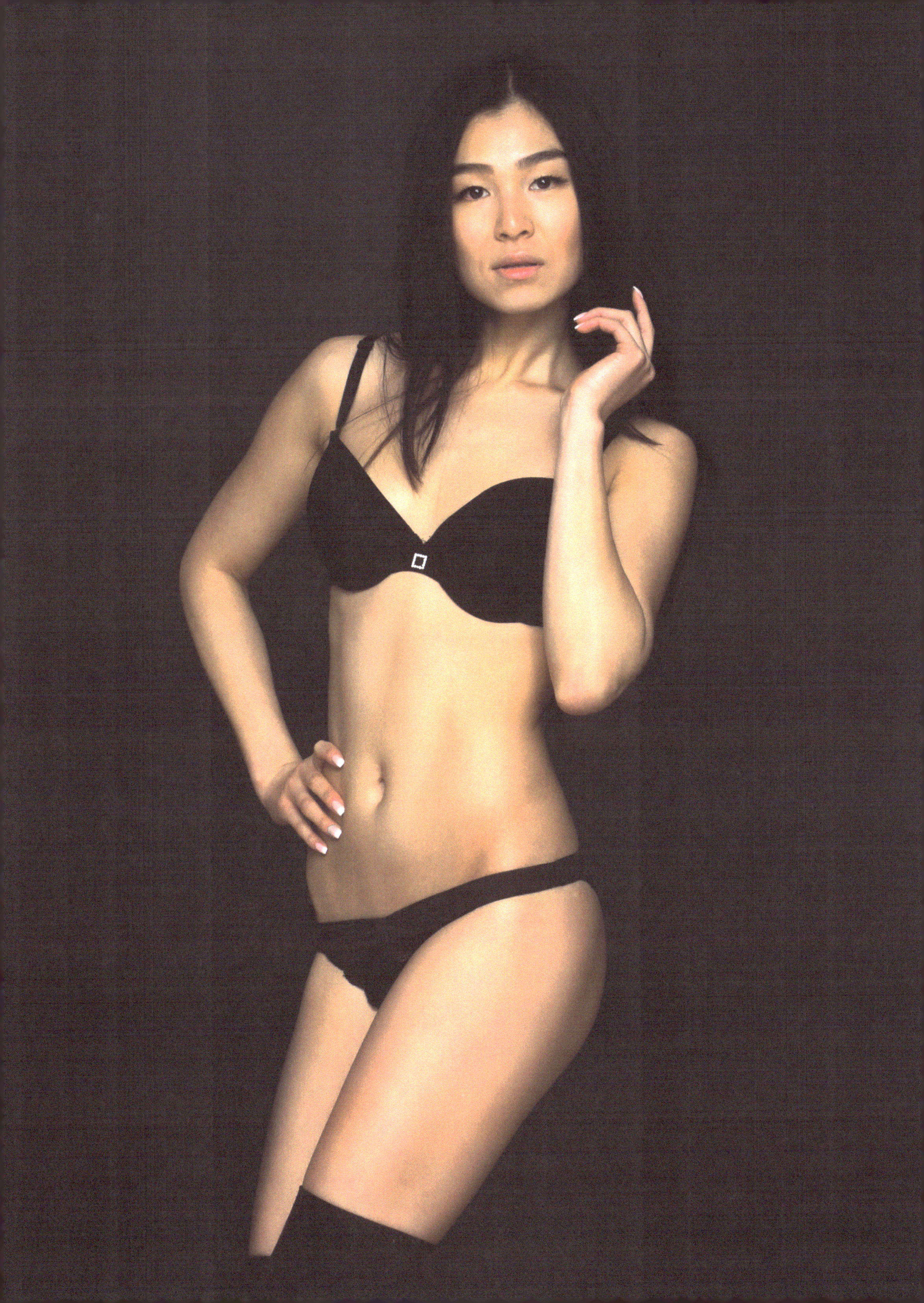

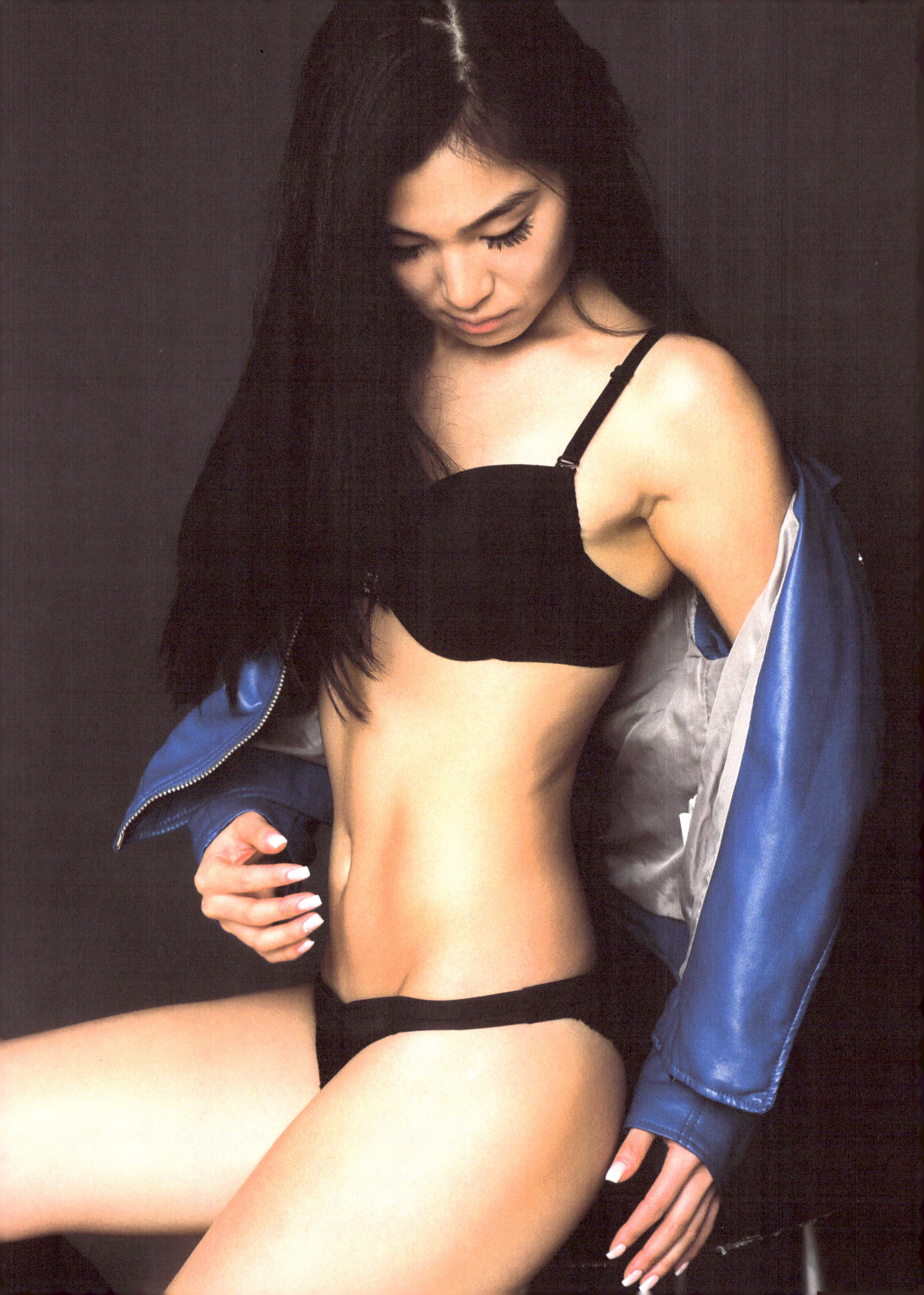

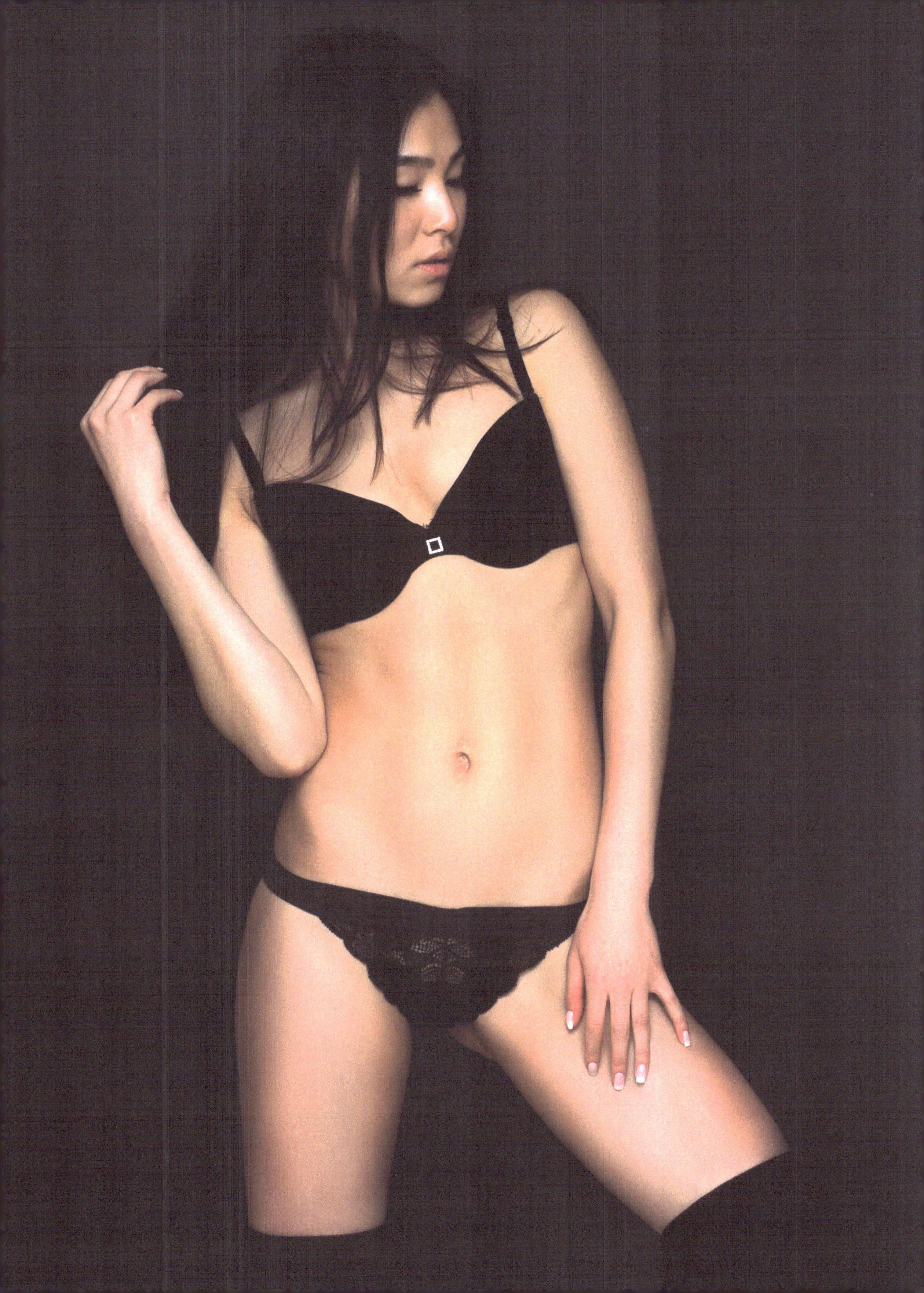

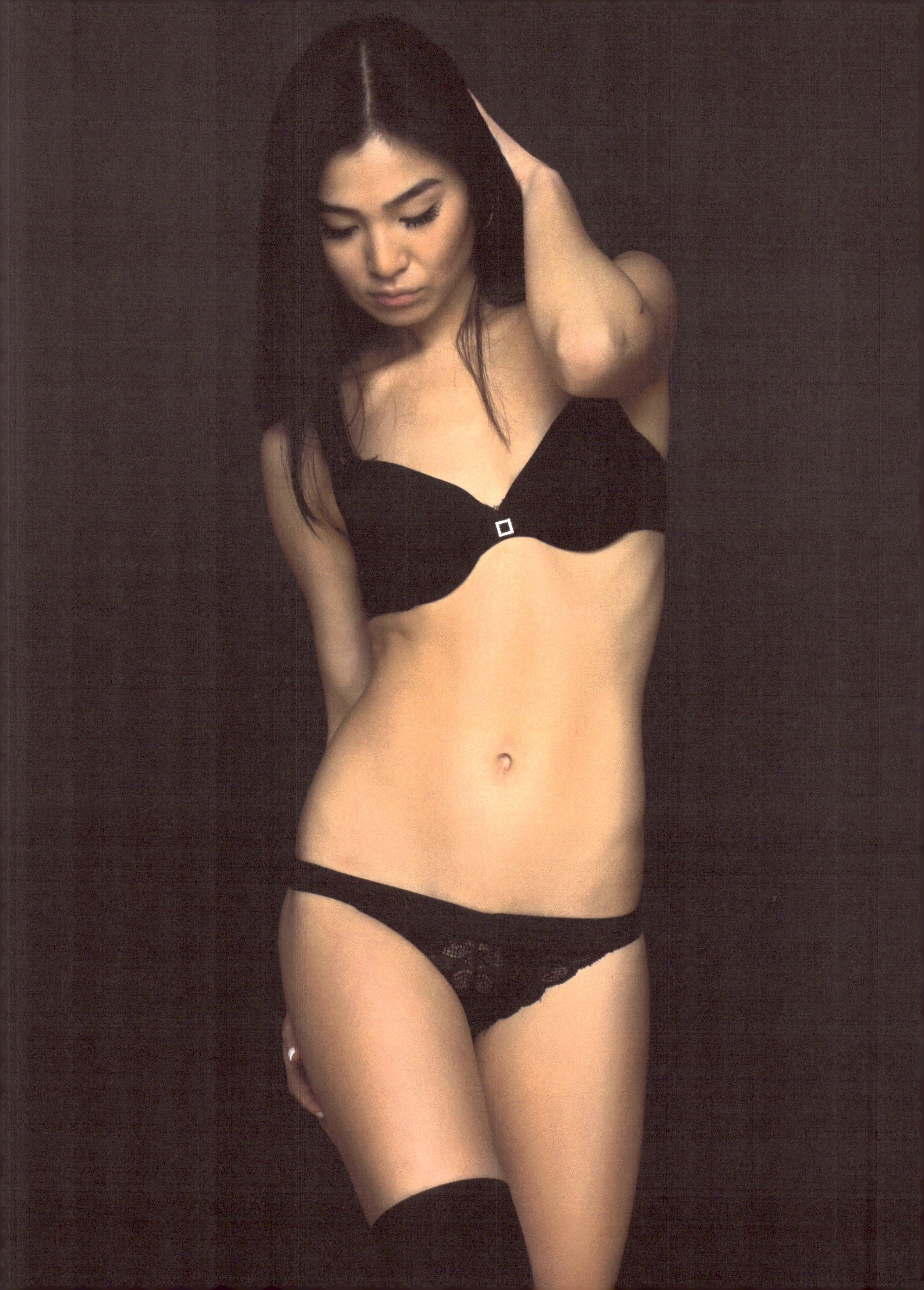

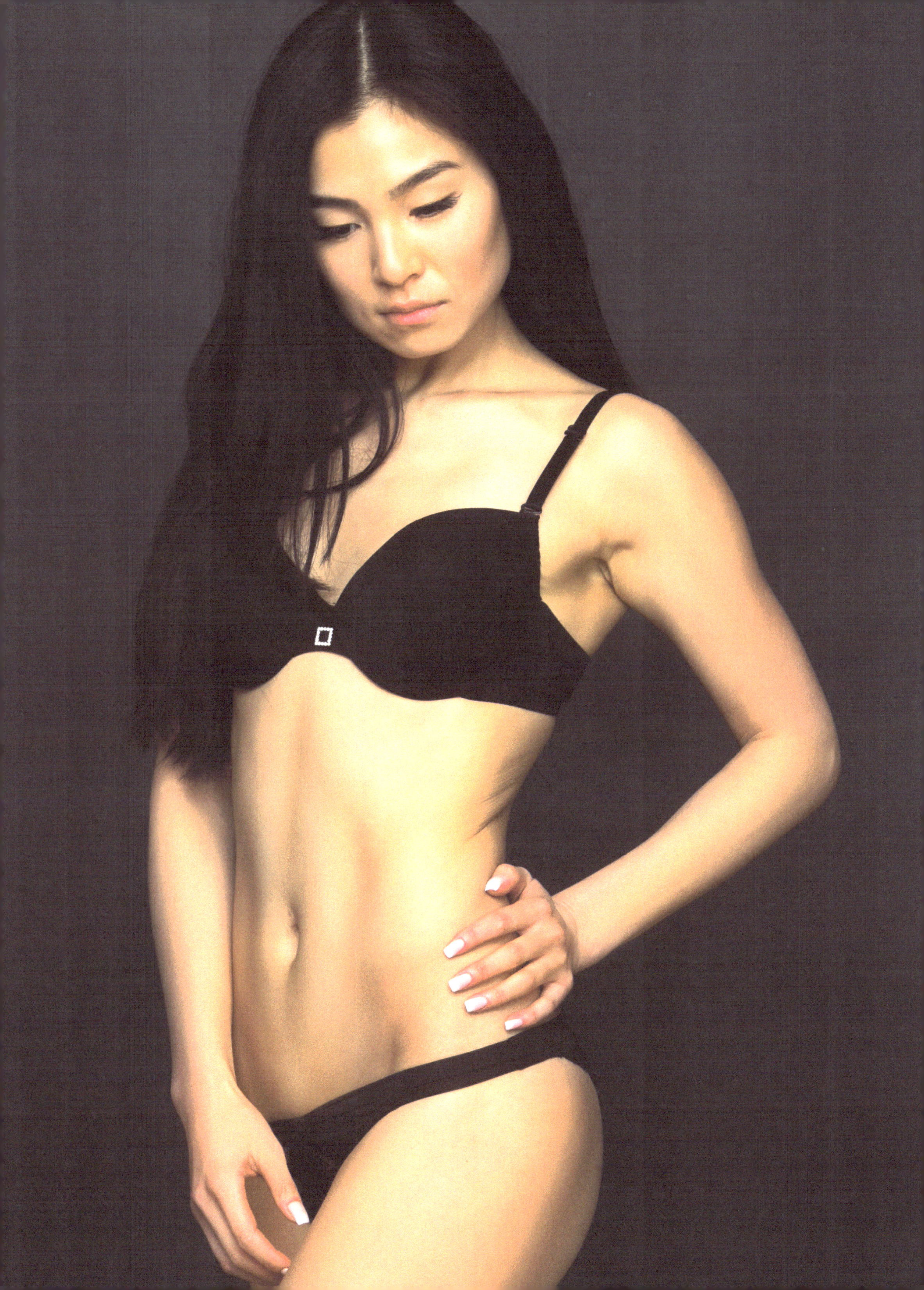

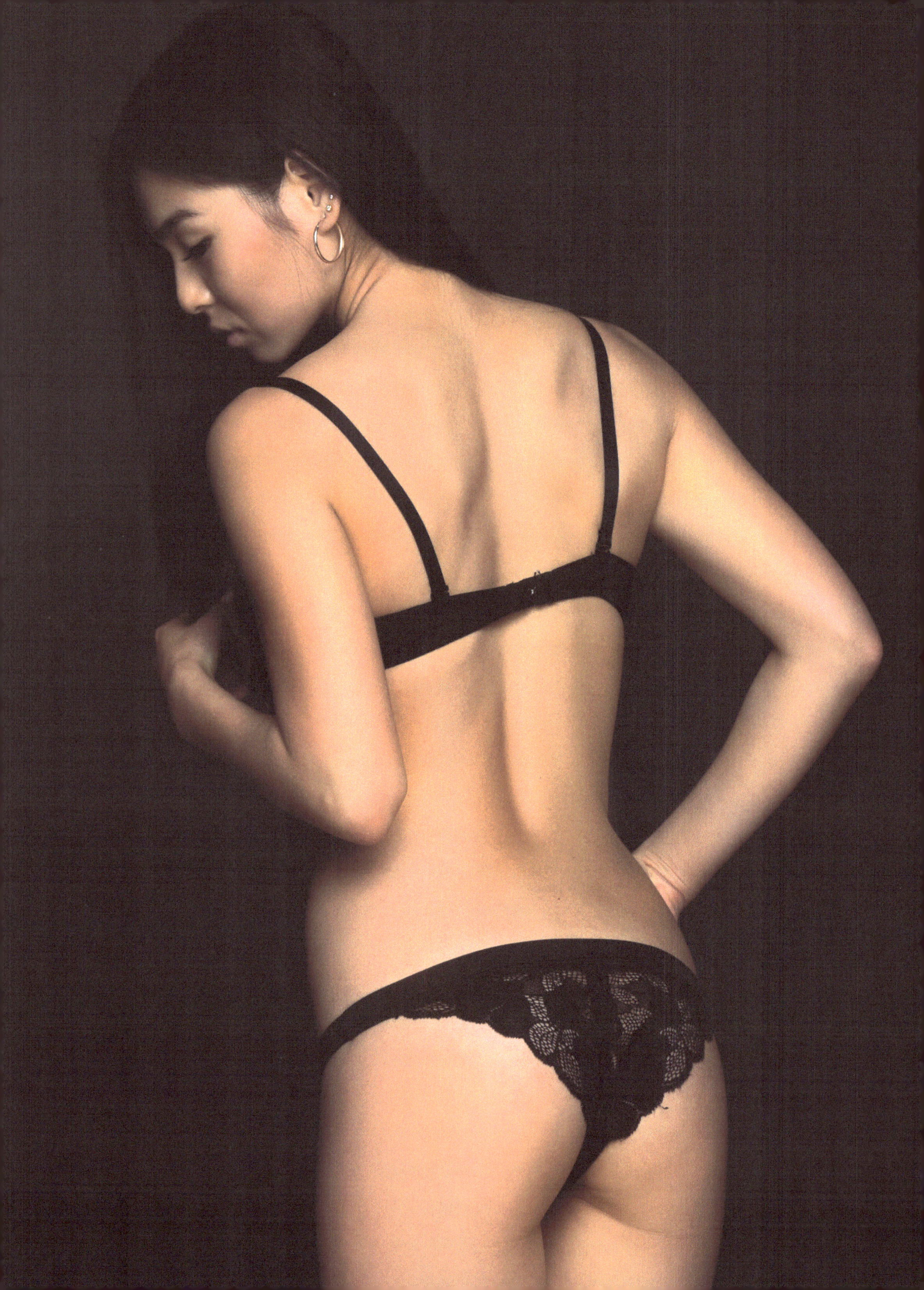

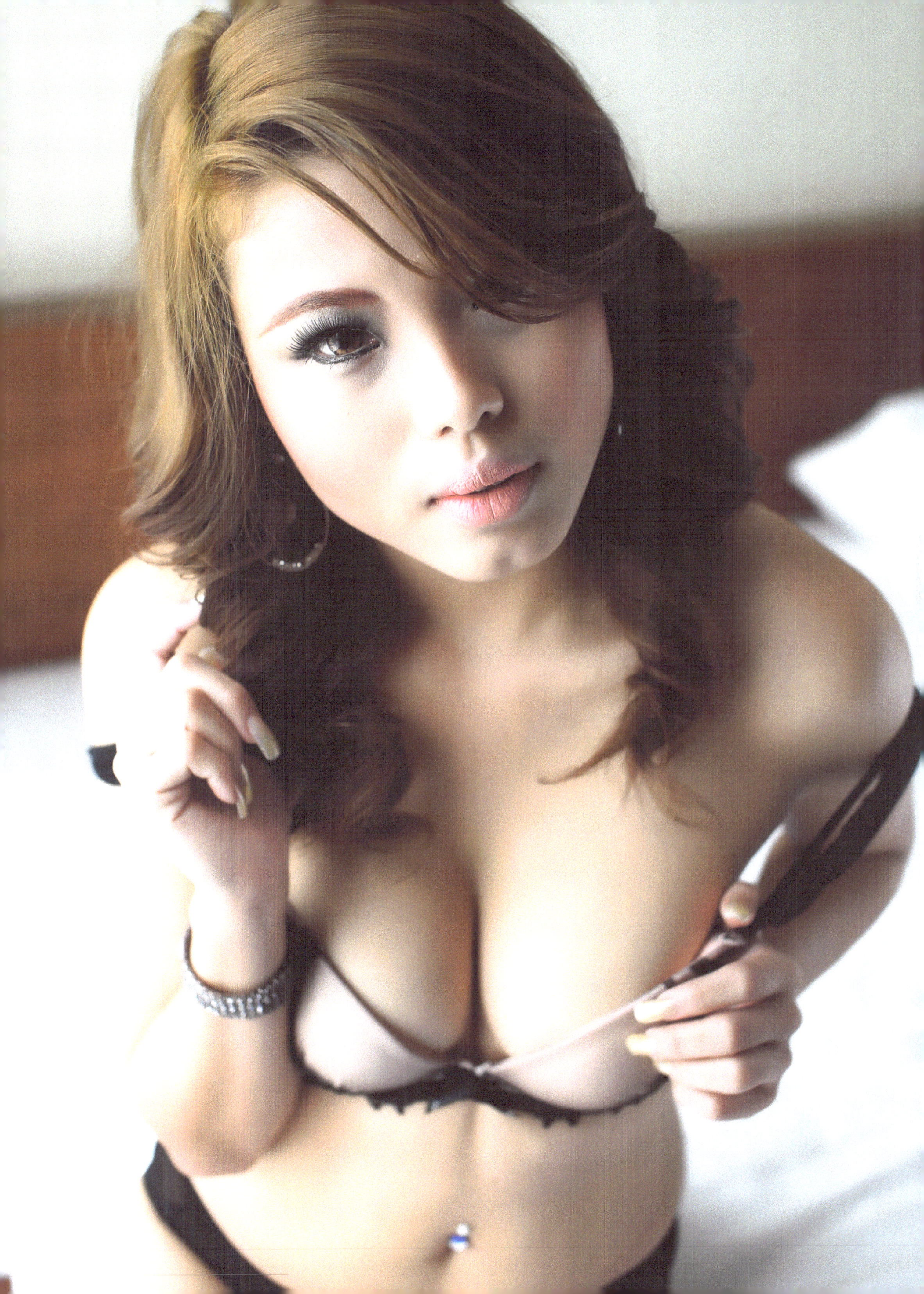

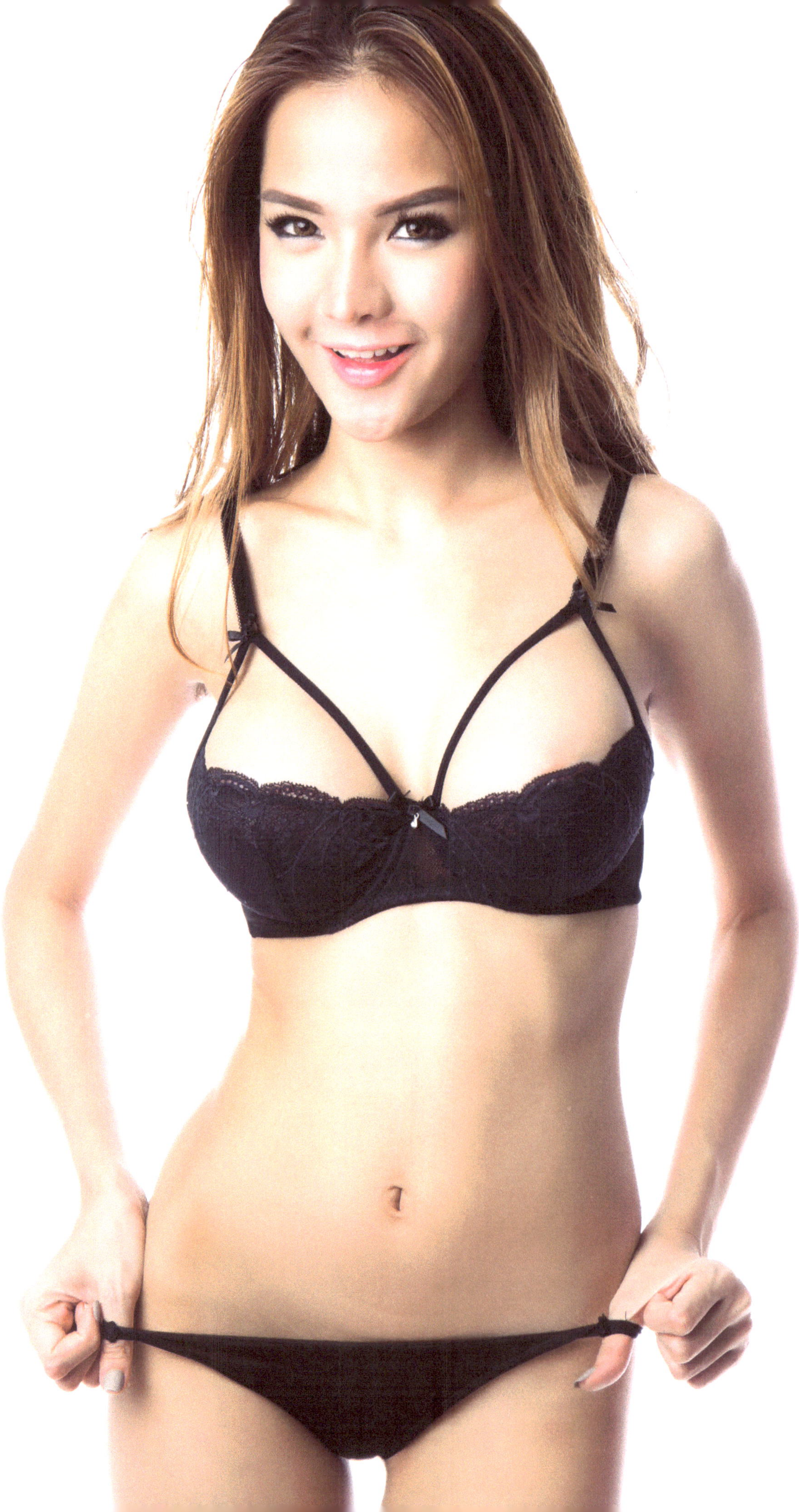

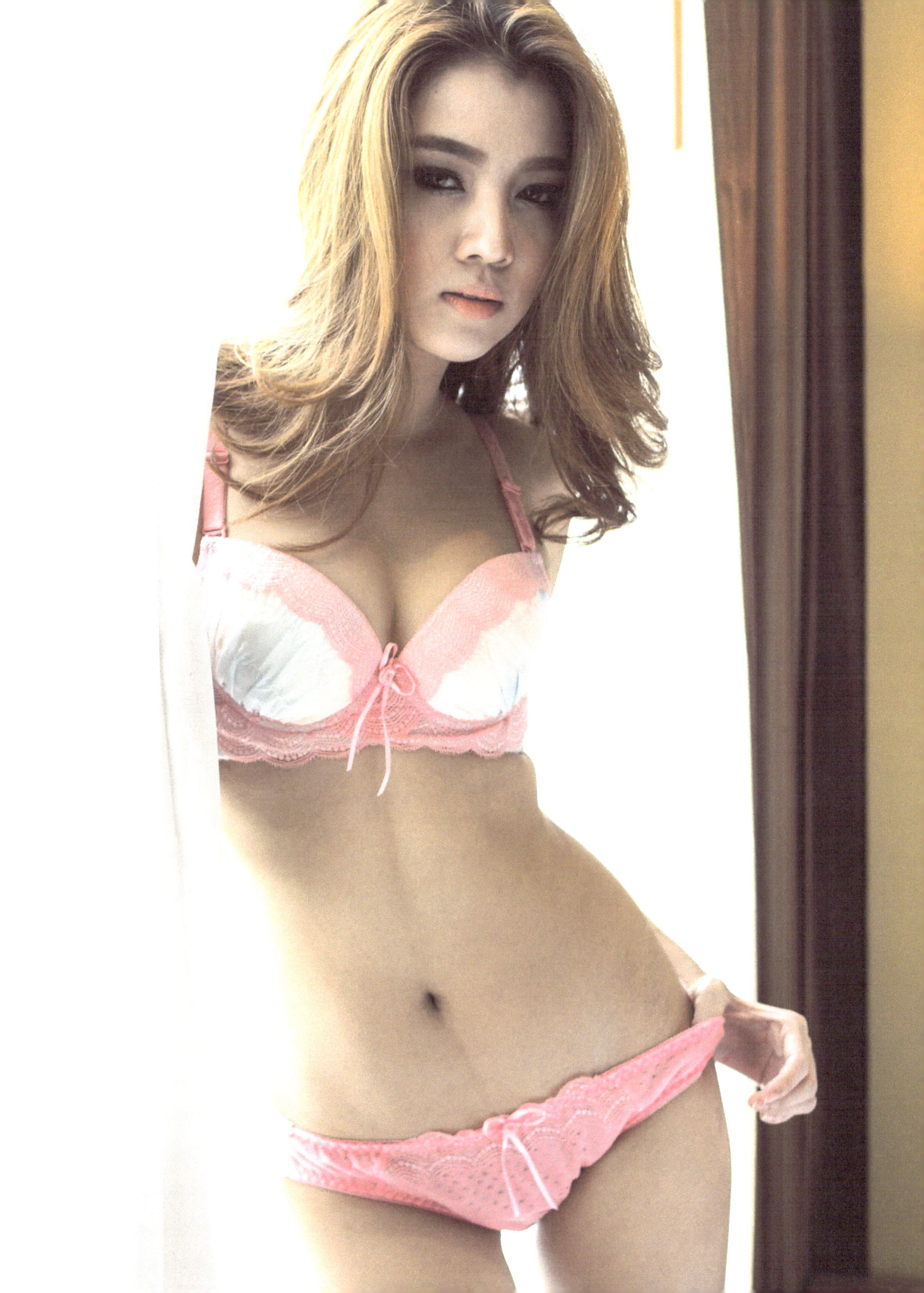

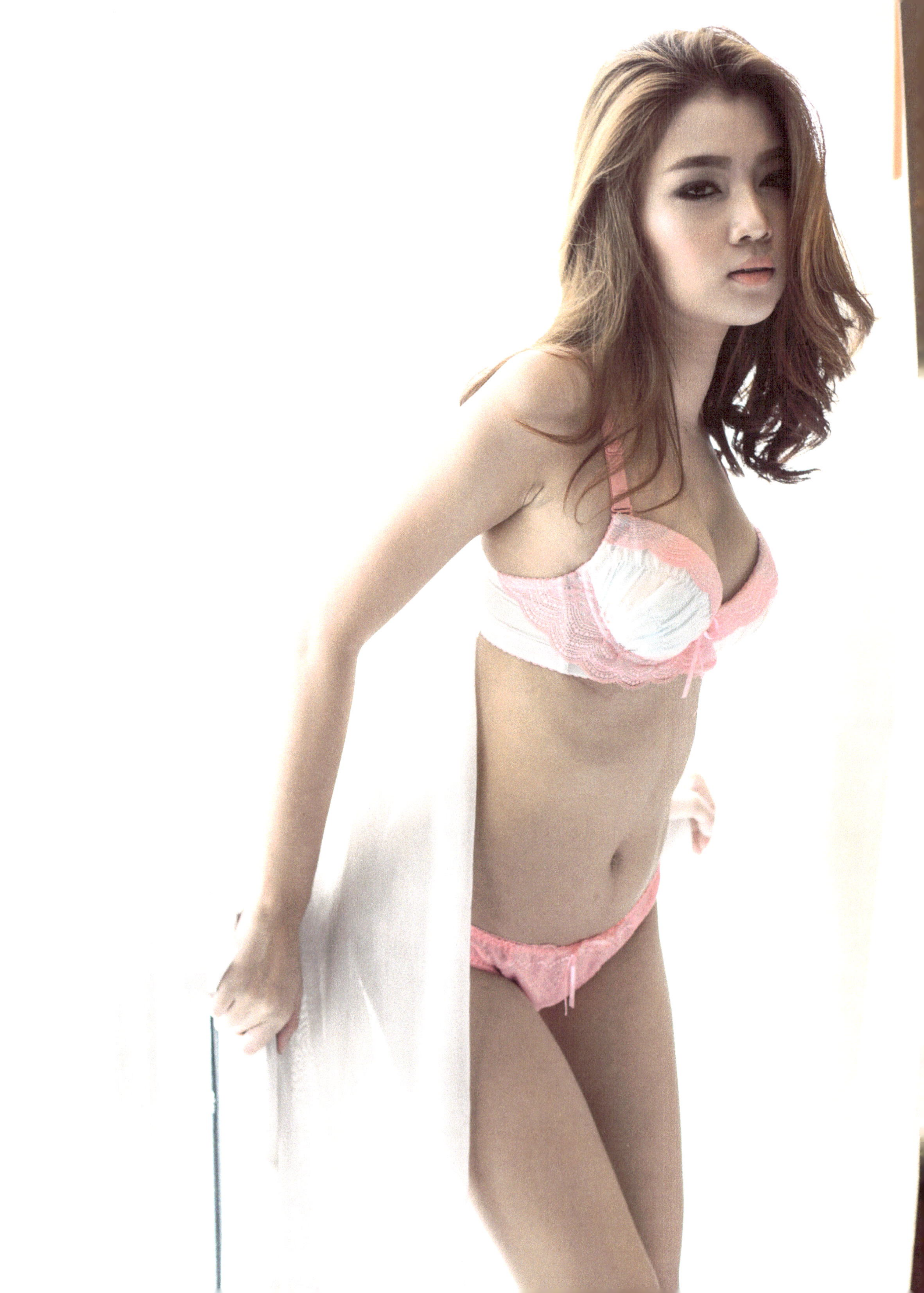

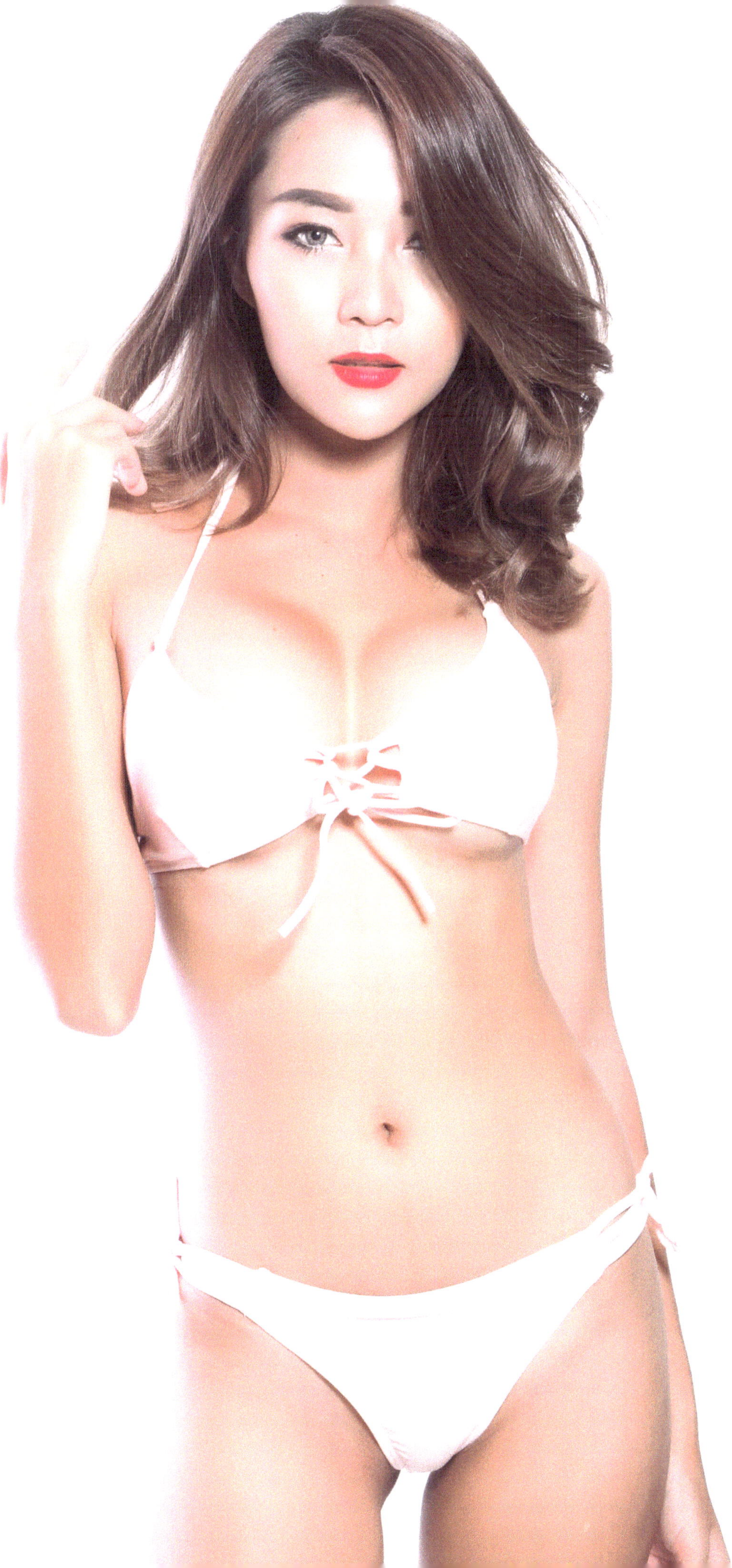

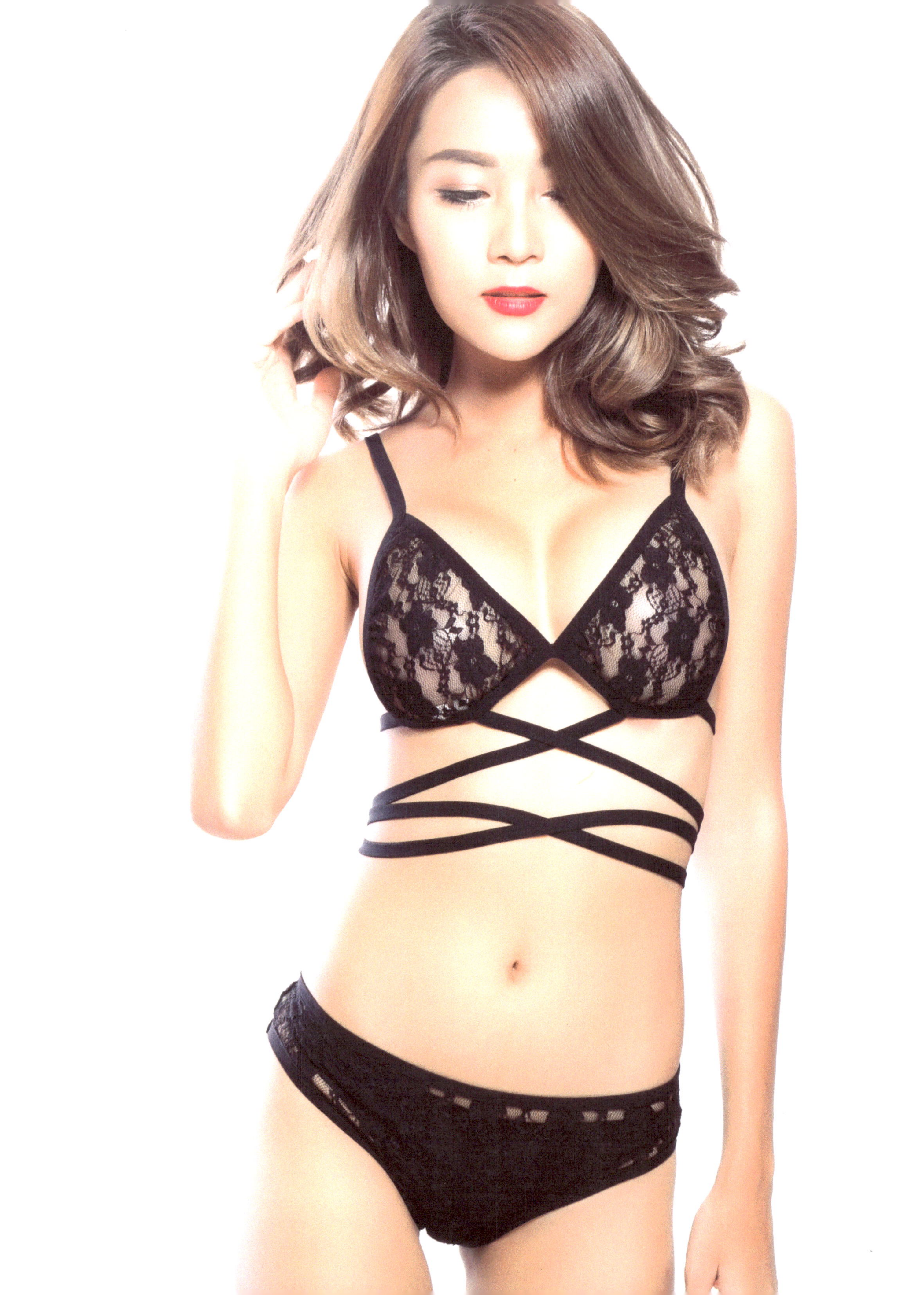

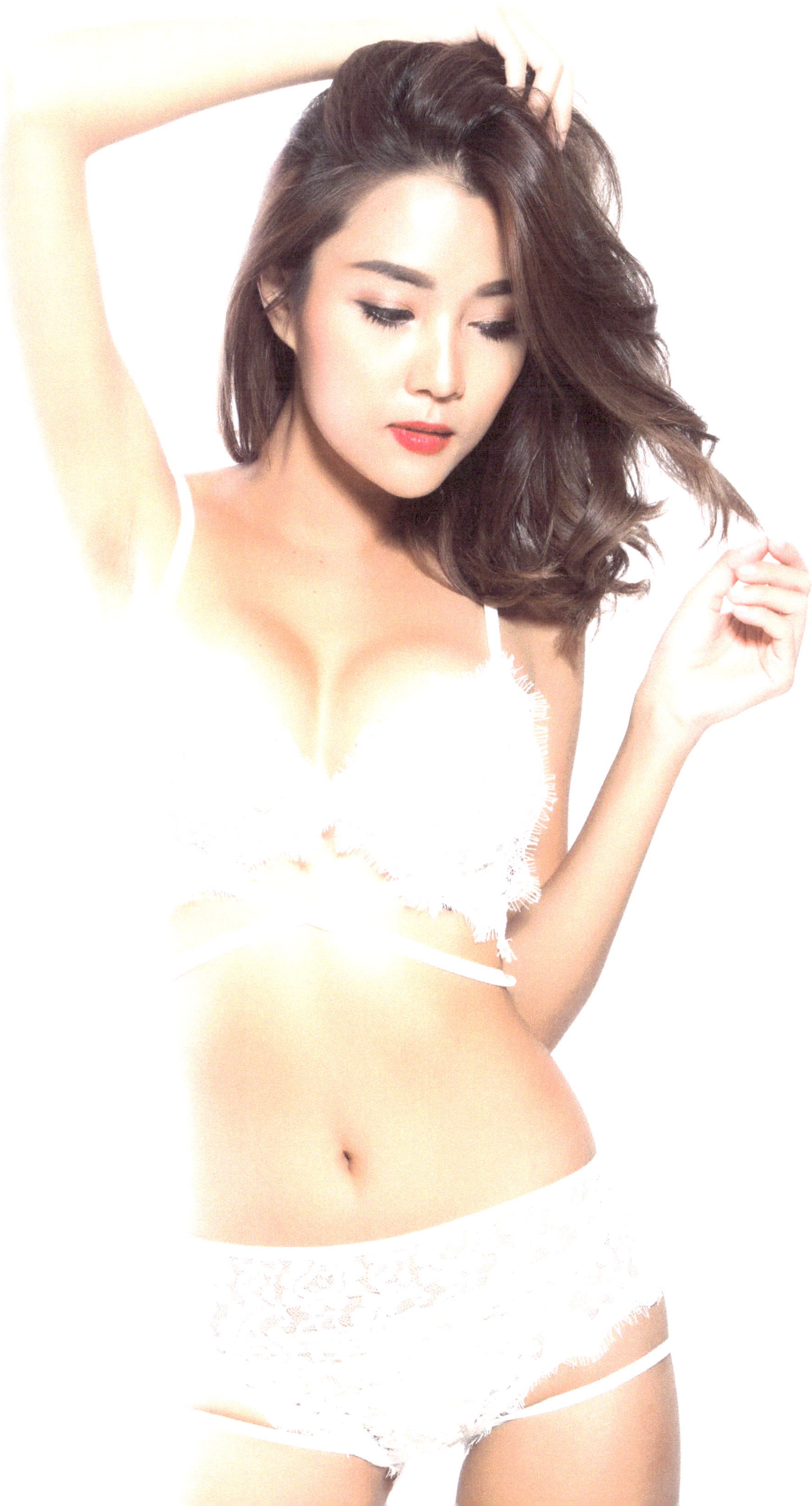

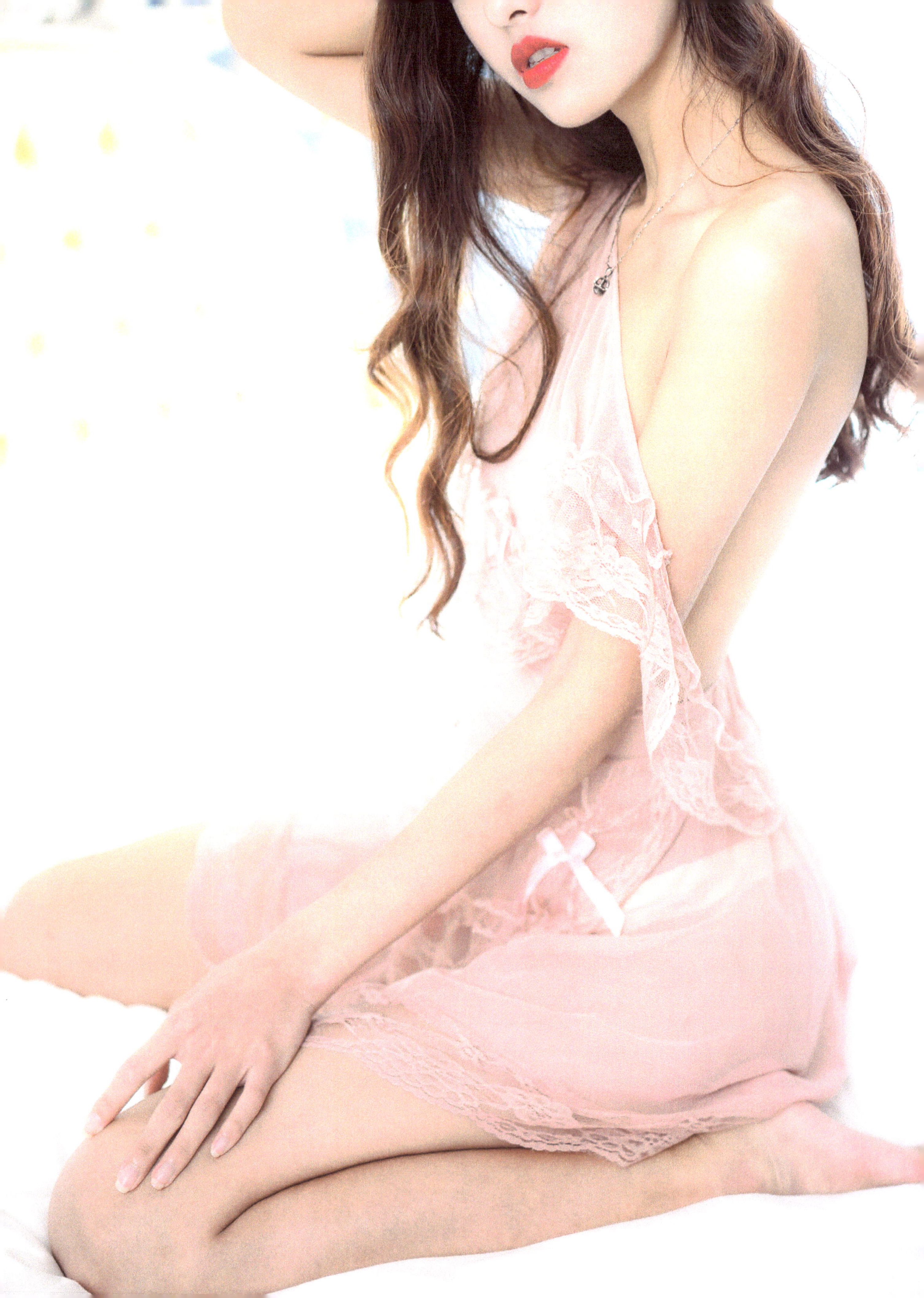

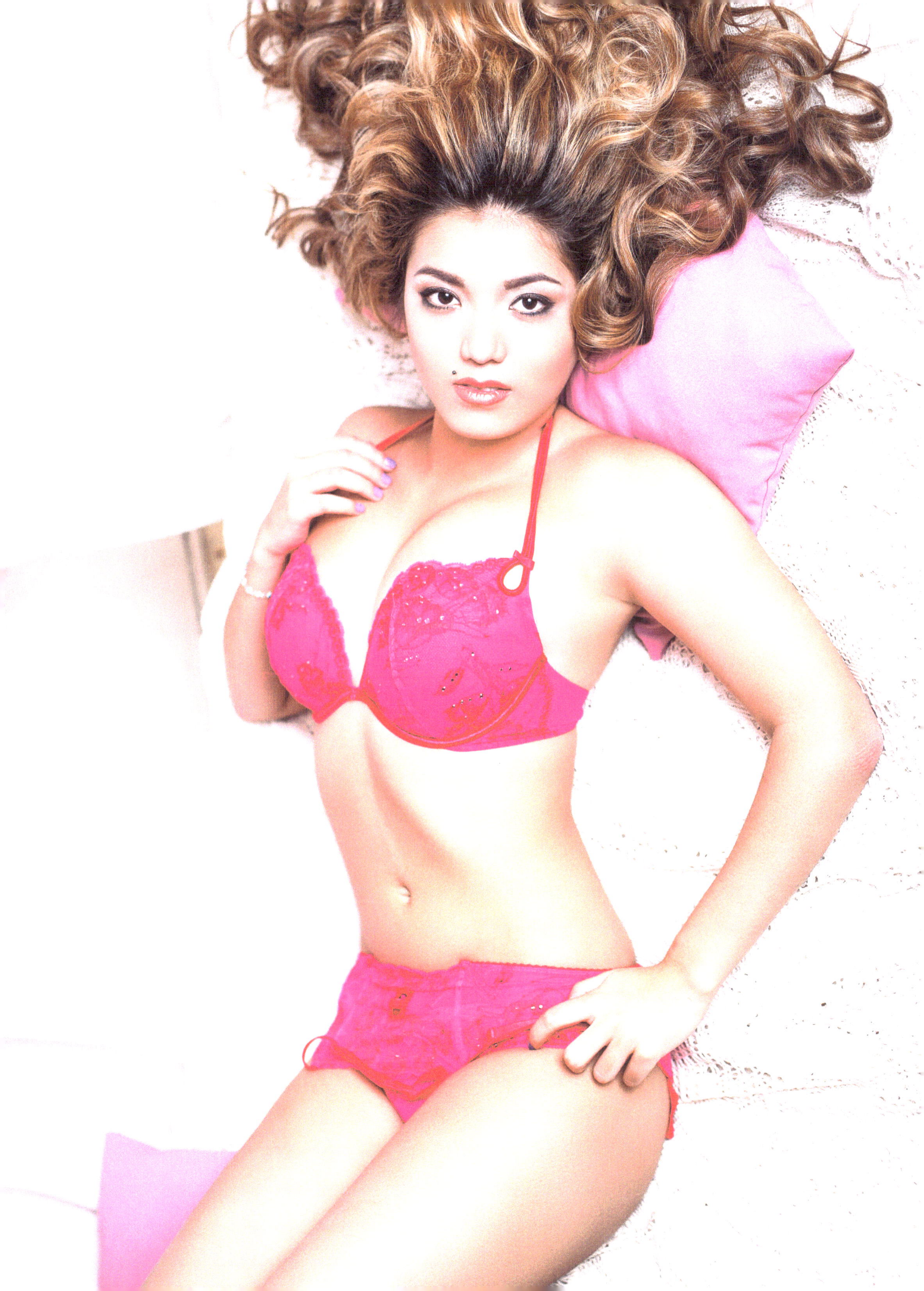

www.ingramcontent.com/pod-product-compliance
Lightning Source LLC
Chambersburg PA
CBHW050418180526
45159CB00005B/2320
* 9 7 8 1 5 3 9 1 0 4 5 1 3 *